Green

Sarah Fleming

contents

can you See Green?

This book is about the color green. Can you see the color green?

Can you see the number in the square below? If not, you may have red-green **color blindness**.

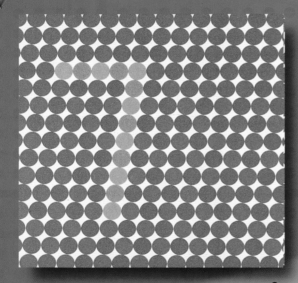

Many people who have red-green color blindness can see more at night than other people. They can also see more shades of some colors than other people.

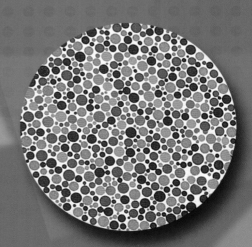

Is Green a Primary color?

Primary colors can be mixed together to make all the other colors. You cannot make a primary color by mixing other colors.

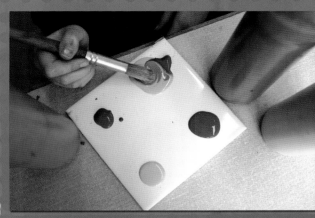

When you mix paint, the primary colors are:
- red,
- yellow,
- blue.

In paint, green is made up of yellow and blue, so green is *not* a primary color.

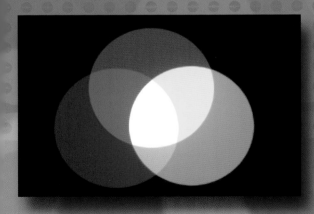

When you mix light, though, the primary colors are:
- red,
- blue,
- green.

In light, yellow is made up of green and red, so green *is* a primary color.

Green Is Restful

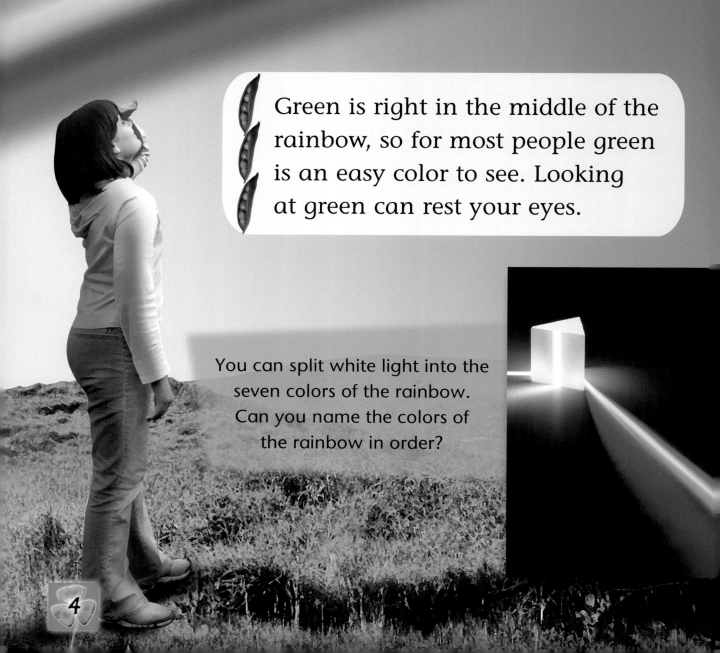

Green is right in the middle of the rainbow, so for most people green is an easy color to see. Looking at green can rest your eyes.

You can split white light into the seven colors of the rainbow. Can you name the colors of the rainbow in order?

The Romans knew that green was good for the eyes. The emperor Nero looked through a green gemstone to watch gladiators fight.

The gemstone was an emerald.

AD 60

Monks used to paint tiny pictures in their books. This made their eyes hurt, so they sometimes looked at a green stone to rest their eyes.

The green stone was malachite.

AD 1100–1300

A hundred years ago, the stage lights in theaters were bright gaslights. When actors looked at them for a long time, their eyes hurt. The actors needed to rest their eyes. The room they rested in was painted green.

Gaslights were used on stage from 1870 to 1930.

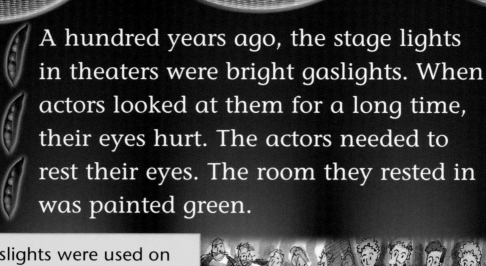

Today, the room where actors rest backstage is still called the Green Room.

Green and Red

Some gardeners use color in a pleasing way. For example, they make long, green, leafy paths...

...that take you around a corner or through a gap...

Look at this picture for 30 seconds. Then turn the page...

If you say someone has "green fingers," what does it mean?

WOW!

... and you see brightly colored flowers. Your eyes have rested with the green, so the bright colors of the flowers seem brighter.

Look at the green dot for 20 seconds. Then look at the white box. What do you see?

Red and green are on opposite sides of the color wheel. This is why they contrast well.

Green means different things in different places. What does it mean in these places?

What is the opposite of green in all these places?

9

Why Are Plants Green?

Most plants on Earth are green. They are green because they have **chlorophyll** (say "klor-uh-fill") in them. The chlorophyll takes in light from the sun. It uses the light to make food for the plant.

Sun

Light from the sun

In some plants, the chlorophyll dies in the autumn, so the leaves lose their green color. Then you can see the other colors in the leaves.

While the plant is making food, it is also giving out **oxygen**. Oxygen makes up 20 percent of air on Earth. All living things need oxygen.

Oxygen into the air

Green leaf

Plant

How a plant makes oxygen

Green rain forests make lots of oxygen. If they are all cut down, the climate of the Earth will change.

How Green Are You?

Many things in **nature** are green. So if you do things that are good for nature and the **environment**, you say you're being "green."

How many of these things do you **recycle**?

Plastic

Glass bottles

Paper

Plastic bags

Cans

Do you:
- throw your litter into trash cans?
- recycle what you can?
- help clean up local parks?
- turn off the water while you brush your teeth?

Greenpeace is a group that works to protect nature. In this picture, people from Greenpeace are painting on logs. They want to stop an old-growth forest from being cut down.

Green Party

There are Green Parties in politics all around the world. They want to make laws to stop pollution, to save the land, and to protect wild animals.

Yucky Greens!

Green can be yucky.

Snot is green.

Pus is green.

Mold is green.

Slime is green.

Do you know what the "green-eyed monster" is?

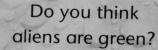

Do you think aliens are green?

14

Look Back

1. Where is green in the rainbow?

2. What do you mix green light with to make yellow light?

3. Why are plants green?

4. Name three things you can recycle.

Index

Glossary

chlorophyll — a chemical in leaves that helps plants change sunlight into energy

color blindness — when a person can't see one or more colors

environment — the land, water, and air around you, and everything that grows on and in it

mold — a furry growth that can appear when some things begin to decay (break down)

nature — things that are alive on Earth

oxygen — a gas that we need to live

primary color — a color that cannot be made from other colors, and is used to make other colors

pus — a thick, yellowy-green liquid that can come out of a sore or a pimple

recycle — to use again

slime — slippery mud, decaying plants, or a liquid made by some animals, such as fish and snails